WHAT IS A GIRAFFE JUICE WORK BOOK?

The Giraffe Juice Work book was created to offer a fun and entertaining way for parents and teachers to share Nonviolent Communication (NVC) with young people (we had the ages 8-12 in mind). It can be enjoyed at home or in the classroom as the companion workbook to Giraffe Juice: The Magic of Making Life Wonderful. Either book can be read first as a complement to the other.

Our vision is to share the peacemaking skills of Giraffe language with over a million people throughout the world by January 1, 2012.

If you would enjoy supporting us, please share our free e-books with anyone you want. Both Giraffe Juice and this companion workbook can be easily accessed for free online at www.GiraffeJuice.com. You can keep all your personal information completely private if that's what you prefer. See the back of this book for more details about how you can share Giraffe Language with anyone you care about.

D0620027

Published by:

Follow Your Joy Press
PO Box 208
Anahola, HI USA 96703

This book is manufactured
in the United States of America.

Giraffe Juice the workbook,
was put together by:

Tania Wolk: Graphic Designer,
Go Giraffe Go Writing & Design Inc.
Brita Lind: Writer,
Go Giraffe Go Writing & Design Inc.
Tamara Laporte:
Cover and interior illustrations

Printed and bound
by Createspace.com

Many thanks to:
Brady Renwick — for trying out the games
and giving us ideas and suggestions.
JP Allen & Marci Winters — for the Giraffe
Juice book that inspired this workbook.
Any teachers and guides out there who
use this book to teach Giraffe Language.

MEET MARVEL

You can find out a new way to talk to the people around you. It uses words you know, but in a different way. It's a language about speaking from your heart and being curious about what's in other people's hearts.

THIS LANGUAGE IS NAMED AFTER AN ANIMAL

Connect the dots to meet that animal!

This animal has a very large heart, about 27 pounds and 2 feet long.

This animal is about 16 feet high, so it sees life differently than you and I.

Other animals like to hang out with this one because they can see things differently.

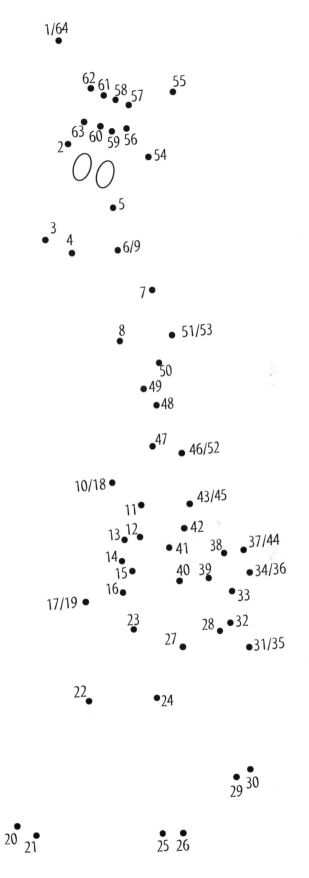

A-MAZING GIRAFFE GAME

Help Eva find her friend Marvel the Giraffe, by **following**

O F N R

in order the four steps of the Giraffe Game: Observations, Feelings, Needs & Requests

E T S D

Stay away from Evaluations, Thoughts, Strategies & Demands

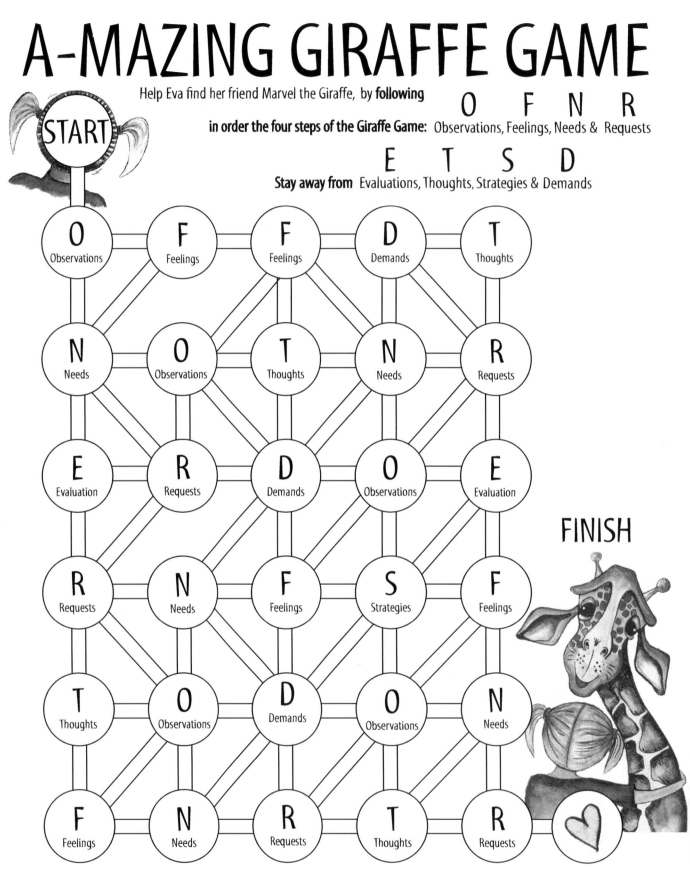

START

O — Observations
F — Feelings
F — Feelings
D — Demands
T — Thoughts

N — Needs
O — Observations
T — Thoughts
N — Needs
R — Requests

E — Evaluation
R — Requests
D — Demands
O — Observations
E — Evaluation

FINISH

R — Requests
N — Needs
F — Feelings
S — Strategies
F — Feelings

T — Thoughts
O — Observations
D — Demands
O — Observations
N — Needs

F — Feelings
N — Needs
R — Requests
T — Thoughts
R — Requests

OBSERVE THE DIFFERENCES

The first step of the Giraffe Game is **Observation.** When you talk about something with your friend or family, **it's important to say <u>exactly what happened</u>** instead of <u>what you think about what happened</u> – which is called an **Evaluation.**

EVALUATION:	GIRAFFE OBSERVATION:
"You suck at bringing my game back." ⟶	"The last time I lent you my game, you didn't give it back."
"You are a liar." ⟶	"You said you left the game on my desk, but I don't see it."

Which statements are a conversation you want to be part of?

INSTRUCTIONS:
Practice your observation skills. Find the 10 differences, in the two almost identical pictures.

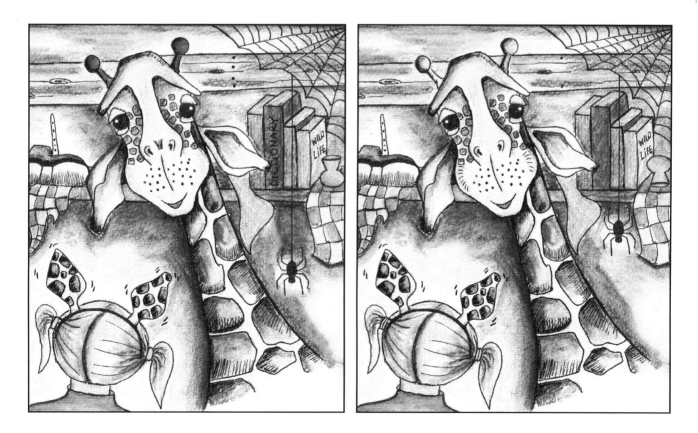

FEELING FINDER

Step 2 of the Giraffe Game. There are many words that pretend to be like feelings, but really they're not. Find out which are which!

DIRECTIONS:

Get two pencil crayons – one light and one a bit darker. Using the light pencil crayon, color in the *true* feeling words – and use the darker pencil crayon for the *false* feeling words. When you're done, you'll see a picture!

TRUE FEELING WORDS

Are about me and how I'm feeling.
EXAMPLES:
- happy
- curious
- tired
- joyful
- lonely
- hurt

FALSE FEELING WORDS

Are about what I think others are doing to me.
EXAMPLES:
- bullied
- blamed
- trapped
- rejected
- betrayed
- left out

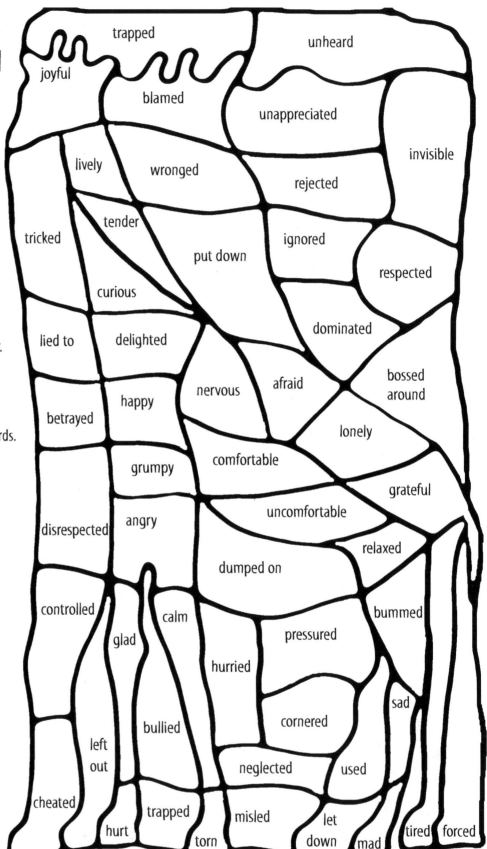

joyful, trapped, unheard, blamed, unappreciated, lively, wronged, invisible, rejected, tender, tricked, put down, ignored, respected, curious, lied to, delighted, dominated, nervous, afraid, bossed around, happy, betrayed, lonely, grumpy, comfortable, grateful, angry, uncomfortable, disrespected, relaxed, dumped on, controlled, bummed, calm, glad, pressured, hurried, sad, bullied, cornered, left out, neglected, used, cheated, trapped, misled, let down, tired, forced, hurt, torn, mad

GIRAFFE WORD SEARCH

Circle all of the bolded giraffe words. They're forward, backward, up and down. Circle the leftover letters and put them in the blanks to find out what Marvel is saying.

D	N	H	E	A	R	T	E	E	N
N	S	E	F	F	A	R	I	G	O
A	T	F	D	E	S	M	N	A	I
M	H	I	R	E	Q	U	E	S	T
E	G	L	B	L	A	M	E	S	A
D	U	C	K	I	T	T	D	N	V
Y	O	P	I	N	I	O	N	I	R
E	H	E	R	G	N	O	R	W	E
S	T	R	A	T	E	G	I	E	S
G	N	I	N	E	T	S	I	L	B
C	U	R	I	O	S	I	T	Y	O

Giraffes realize that if we don't care about other people's needs, they may not care about ours. Giraffes like to get their way, but only if it works for other people too because:

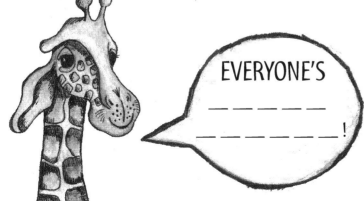

EVERYONE'S

_ _ _ _ _ _
_ _ _ _ _ _ !

Giraffes like to play the Making **LIFE** Wonderful Game a whole lot more than the **BLAME** Game.

In the Blame Game there is always a loser. Giraffes love it when everyone **WINS**.

Giraffes prefer not to use the words "should" and "shouldn't". Sometimes when we use these words others may hear that they are being judged as "**WRONG**."

OBSERVATION. Giraffes use clear observations to describe what they actually hear or see— like what a video camera would record.

Giraffes are careful to not mix their **OPINION** with their observation.

When Giraffes say how they are **FEELING**, they speak about themselves only, and no one else.

Giraffes know the difference between **THOUGHTS** and feelings, and they are careful not to mix them up.

Needs instead of **STRATEGIES**: Food is a need. Broccoli is a strategy. Everyone has a **NEED** for food, but not everyone enjoys broccoli.

GIRAFFES care about the needs of others, not just their own. Asking "would this work for you?" is one way to show that we care about their needs, too.

REQUEST instead of **DEMAND**: Giraffes make requests in a way that allows others to say "**YES**" freely and joyfully like a young child feeding a hungry **DUCK**.

One trick to Giraffe **LISTENING** is to just be silent, while keeping your **CURIOSITY** focused on the other person's feelings and needs.

Giraffe Listening protects you from insults. Instead, you listen for what's in the other person's **HEART.**

GIRAFFE JUMBLE

Before reading the story, fill in the blanks with a word from the matching shape.
Then read your fun story!

FEELINGS
bubbly
happy
sad
hopeful
excited
curious
cheerful
lousy
silly
worried
nervous
full
mad
bored

NOUNS
alien
cheese
bulldozer
pizza
necklace
pencil
wizard
chicken
octopus

VERBS
dance
surf
skip
burp
giggle
swim
splash
wobble
sneeze

NEEDS
play
sleep
fun
water
respect
peace
belonging
choice
love
shelter
warmth
sharing
to learn
celebration

ADJECTIVES
sticky
dull
crispy
spotty
enormous
glittery
slippery
smelly
beautiful
blue

WHAT GIRAFFE JUICE BOOK ALMOST BECAME: INTERVIEW WITH THE AUTHORS

The book, Giraffe Juice was almost named Lion ▢ _____ The Magic of Making ▢ _____ ✦ _____ .

One author, said, "I wrote a ▢ _____ before I felt ● _____ about it." Most readers don't know this, but the

main characters in this book were almost a ✦ _____ lion named ● _____ and a ✦ _____

▢ _____ . But then the authors started feeling ● _____ and decided they needed ★ _____ .

So the authors put a ▢ _____ to paper and started to write the book again. One of the authors turned to the

other and said, "Are you willing to start ▽ _____ ing because I'm feeling ● _____ ?" That started both of

them ▽ _____ ing and the book became a number-one best seller in the world.

HAVE I GOT A GIRAFFE FOR YOU

Giraffes have created the curiosity of ▢ _____ s since the earliest times. The giraffe has ✦ _____ ears

that are sensitive to the faintest ▢ _____ , and it has a ✦ _____ sense of smell and sight. Giraffes have

needs, especially ★ _____ and ★ _____ . Giraffes may appear quite ● _____ , but this is not

always true, it's best to ask first. When attacked, a giraffe can put on a ✦ _____ display by ▽ _____ ing

repeatedly. Also, a giraffe can gallop at more than thirty ▢ _____ s per hour, and can outrun the fastest

▢ _____ .

HOW TO GIVE EMPATHY

If someone you know is feeling ● _____ and you're wondering if you can make their ▢ _____ more

✦ _____ , try empathy. Here's how it ▽ _____ s. Go and talk with your friend and ask, "Are you feeling

● _____ because you are needing ★ _____ ?" And then listen to their answer. You might think they are

feeling ● _____ . But that's ok, because you care about what's going on for them. If they answer, "No, I'm feeling

● _____ because I am needing ★ _____ ," that's great! Just ▽ _____ your ✦ _____

ears as you listen and when they finish what they say, you can say, "Wow, I feel so ● _____ hearing what you just

said." You don't have to tell your friend to stop being so ✦ _____ . Just listening to them will help you

▽ _____ with their heart.

NEED SEARCH

Step 3 is about needs. **Needs are universal, meaning that all human beings share the same needs.**

Look forward, backward, up, down, diagonal, sideways, reverse and every which way.

S	P	A	C	E	X	E	R	C	I	S	E	M	A	T	T	E	R	I	N	G
H	W	C	O	O	P	E	R	A	T	I	O	N	E	Q	U	A	L	I	T	Y
E	O	Y	C	O	N	N	E	C	T	I	O	N	E	F	R	E	E	D	O	M
L	C	P	Y	W	U	N	D	E	R	S	T	A	N	D	I	N	G	Q	U	I
T	L	O	E	A	A	B	Y	X	Z	S	E	L	F	R	E	S	P	E	C	T
E	J	J	M	B	P	T	H	S	P	O	N	T	A	N	E	I	T	Y	H	S
R	S	O	C	M	U	P	E	A	C	C	E	P	T	A	N	C	E	I	C	H
H	L	L	B	A	U	N	R	F	O	O	D	H	A	R	M	O	N	Y	T	P
I	N	D	E	P	E	N	D	E	N	C	E	S	Y	N	G	T	H	W	I	L
T	F	B	L	E	H	C	I	J	C	I	U	T	U	N	S	T	O	H	A	A
Y	S	O	O	L	P	R	B	C	Q	I	I	F	I	U	A	R	S	W	C	Y
C	T	H	N	M	E	E	X	T	A	R	A	R	R	P	G	N	S	A	O	A
H	I	O	G	O	P	A	I	R	A	T	U	T	M	U	O	I	U	R	M	F
A	M	N	I	V	R	T	R	L	P	T	I	E	I	I	T	N	P	M	P	F
L	U	E	N	E	E	I	C	N	R	U	Y	O	N	O	E	C	P	T	A	E
L	L	S	G	M	S	V	N	U	I	T	R	A	N	S	N	L	O	H	S	C
E	A	T	L	E	E	I	N	D	E	N	P	P	A	D	W	U	R	U	S	T
N	T	Y	O	N	N	T	E	F	T	M	G	E	O	I	A	S	T	M	I	I
G	I	Y	V	T	C	Y	A	S	O	R	D	E	R	S	T	I	T	O	O	O
E	O	R	E	Q	E	S	E	C	C	H	O	I	C	E	E	O	B	R	N	N
R	N	C	O	N	T	R	I	B	U	T	I	O	N	R	R	N	Z	R	E	I

acceptance	communication	equality	humor	order	space
air	companionship	exercise	inclusion	play	spontaneity
appreciation	compassion	freedom	independence	presence	stimulation
affection	connection	food	joy	purpose	support
beauty	contribution	fun	learning	rest	touch
belonging	cooperation	growth	love	safety	trust
challenge	creativity	harmony	mattering	selfrespect	understanding
choice	ease	honesty	movement	shelter	warmth
clarity	empathy	hope	nurturing	sleep	water

WHAT'S IN YOUR HEART?

Another special part of Giraffe Language is empathy. Empathy is about guessing what other people are feeling and needing in order to connect with them and listen to them with your heart. The "What's in Your Heart Game?" is a fun way to practice empathy.

Instructions are on the other side.

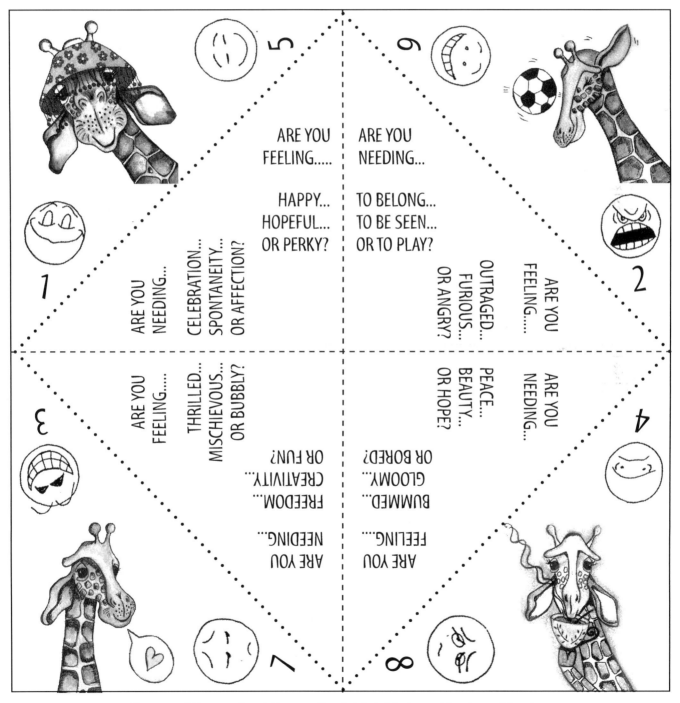

ARE YOU FEELING.....

HAPPY... HOPEFUL... OR PERKY?

ARE YOU NEEDING...

TO BELONG... TO BE SEEN... OR TO PLAY?

ARE YOU NEEDING... CELEBRATION... SPONTANEITY... OR AFFECTION?

OUTRAGED... FURIOUS... OR ANGRY? ARE YOU FEELING.....

ARE YOU FEELING..... THRILLED... MISCHIEVOUS... OR BUBBLY?

PEACE... BEAUTY... OR HOPE? ARE YOU NEEDING...

FREEDOM... CREATIVITY... OR FUN? ARE YOU NEEDING...

BUMMED... GLOOMY... OR BORED? ARE YOU FEELING...

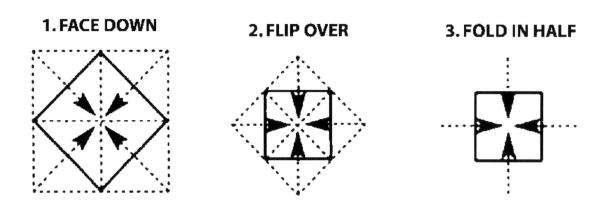

1. FACE DOWN

2. FLIP OVER

3. FOLD IN HALF

1. CUT along the solid lines.
2. ILLUSTRATIONS FACING DOWN - Fold all four corners together so that they meet in the middle of the paper, crease firmly and leave them there.
3. FLIP OVER - Again fold all four corners together so that they meet in the centre of the paper, give a good crease and leave them there.
4. FOLD in half in one direction, then in half in the other direction.
5. FINISH - Stick your thumbs and first two fingers into the four pockets on the bottom of the folded paper and start moving them back and forth to begin the game.

TO PLAY WITH A FRIEND
1. Spell their name and open and close the game with each letter.
2. Ask them to pick one of the faces or numbers they see. Open and close the game that many times.
3. Then ask your friend to pick one of the new faces they see.
4. Lift the flap they picked and ask the empathy question.

what's in your heart?

"Empathy, can sometimes be that wonderful warm experience of sensing that someone else is deeply connecting with us and accepting us as we are."
—page 63, Giraffe Juice: The Magic of Making Life Wonderful

FEELINGS & NEEDS

Here's a way you can practice what's a feeling and what's a need. Look at the list of needs in the middle and match them up with how you might feel when each need is met or unmet for you. There are no right or wrong answers. Have fun!

WHEN NEEDS ARE MET FEELINGS	UNIVERSAL NEEDS	WHEN NEEDS ARE NOT MET FEELINGS

I feel _____ when my need for _____ is met. When my need for _____ is not met I feel _____ .

WHEN NEEDS ARE MET FEELINGS	UNIVERSAL NEEDS	WHEN NEEDS ARE NOT MET FEELINGS
happy	CHOICE	tired
confident	FUN	sad
refreshed	BELONGING	restless
grateful	AFFECTION	cranky
hopeful	LEARNING	worried
joyful	REST	fragile
relaxed	TRUST	annoyed
amazed	UNDERSTANDING	bored
enjoy	COMPASSION	upset
calm	EASE	bummed
relieved	TO MATTER	Irritated
delighted	TO BE HEARD	uneasy
peaceful	SPACE	cautious
awesome	FREEDOM	scared
fascinated	CLARITY	hostile
thankful	CONNECTION	gloomy
confident	FRIENDSHIP	afraid
bubbly	WELLNESS	disappointed
energized	SAFETY	ashamed
friendly	CELEBRATION	confused
thrilled	SHARING	freaked out
excited	HELP	distracted
wonder	HONESTY	jealous

HOW TO TALK LIKE A GIRAFFE

Sometimes, we play the "Blame Game" inside ourselves with blame, labels and judgments. In Giraffe Language, you can turnaround the words you say to yourself. It's called self-empathy. **To practice, take a Blame Game statement and match it to what a Giraffe can say.**

BLAME GAME
(LABELS AND JUDGMENTS)

GIRAFFE LANGUAGE
(SELF-EMPATHY)

I'm letting everyone down.

I'm such a klutz.

I'm just a kid.

I'm smarter than you.

I'll never get it right.

I shouldn't have done that.

- I'm sad about what I said to my friend and I need peace between us.

- I'm feeling frustrated I didn't help and I'm needing it to be more clear about how I can help.

- I'm feeling sad about how my homework has gone today and I'm needing support and understanding.

- I feel sad when they don't let me help because I am needing to contribute.

- I'm scared to try something new and I'm needing some understanding and support before I try something new.

- I'm happy about how I did on the last test and I need to celebrate.

The Blame Game is about putting people in two different groups: Who is good/Who is bad...Who is right/Who is wrong...etcetera. The Blame Game does not create peace in our world.

GIRAFFE EARS

In Giraffe Language, listening is really important. When we listen to what other people need, we are listening with our hearts. That helps add to a peaceful world.

INSTRUCTIONS:

1. Color the ears and the headband (if you want).
2. Cut them out, being careful to keep the ears attached to the headband.
3. Cut an extra strip of paper to make your headband long enough to wrap around your head.
4. Glue or tape the ends of the paper together so the headband fits around your head.
5. Now you can go around wiggling your ears and guessing what your friends and family are feeling and needing!

If you want to make more for your friends, just photocopy this page.

we practice again the ... and yesterday? I want to hear what it would be like ... mom talked like ... giraffe."

"... Eva. How about this? I'll make believe I'm your mother with giraffe ears on and you can speak any ..."

Eva shared some ... things that her mom said earlier that day and Marvel jumped right into his ... Mom. "It's time to go to school, Eva. I'm feeling concerned ... time and I'd like to go now." Eva started to grin from cheek to cheek, hearing ... trying to make his voice sound chirpy like her mom.

But she took a breath and focused her attention back to her part in the role-play. She imagined herself standing in the driveway by her mom's car. She decided to act like she was in a bad mood.

"I don't want to go. I don't like all the boring stuff they teach me."

Marvel responded, still making believe "Are you frustrated with what's being taught at school, honey?"

"Yes!" Eva exclaimed. "I'm never going to use the stuff they teach us anyway!"

"Sounds like you're feeling annoyed about studying things that you don't see any point in learning."

"That's right, Mom. And worse than that, they don't teach us the stuff that really matters, like how to get along with other kids. They can't even help me with my problems with Jip."

"Eva, are you feeling disappointed because you want to learn things that really matter to you?"

"Yeah! And I don't like the way adults force me to learn things I don't care about. And then they say something annoying like…" Eva spoke with a whiny mocking voice, "'You'll thank me when you get older Eva'. YUCK! I can't stand that when grown-ups say those kinds of things to me. Things like, 'You're just a kid, and you'll understand someday'."

Marvel's ears started to wiggle and he moved closer to her. "Eva. I'm not sure about this, but do you feel annoyed when grown-ups say those kind of things because…"

Eva jumped in, raising her voice. "It's so annoying, Marvel! Just because I'm younger doesn't mean I don't understand! And it doesn't mean I'm inferior! It really gets on my nerves when grown-ups act like they're superior."

Eva leaned up against the doorframe of the barn and hung her head toward the ground. ... After a while, she noticed Marvel was still standing there listening ... her. She started to relax.

"I know that my mom and dad want to help me. And most of the time they do. But sometimes I wish they would listen to what I have to say before they make me do things I don't want to do.

"It's hard for me because, whenever I get angry, I really don't want to listen to a word they have to say and I know that only makes things worse. Could we do another practice round, Marvel, where I get to be the giraffe and I practice listening?"

THE GOAL OF GIRAFFE LANGUAGE IS TO....

Finish the sentences to discover the hidden message. The answers to this word game can be found throughout this book, if you need some clues to solve the puzzles unscramble the words below. Go giraffe...go!

Everyone's needs . . . .
     R T M E A T

Asking "would this work for you?" is one way to show others that we... . . . .
     E A C R

Saying "yes" freely and joyfully is like a child feeding a hungry . . . .
     U D K C

Something universal we all share . . . .
     E D N S E

In the Blame Game there is always a . . . .
     E S R O L

Describing what you actually hear and see is called an . . .
     A I S E N B R O V O T

Instead of thoughts, giraffes talk about their . . . .
     S I E G N E F L

When giraffes ask for exactly what they want it's called a . . . .
     E R Q S T U E

In the Blame Game, people think in terms of right and . . . .
     R G N W O

Giraffes share observations rather than . . . .
     I I N N O O P

Listening like a Giraffe protects you from . . . .
     T U S N L S I

A request instead of a _____ allows others to say "yes" . . . .
     M A D D E N

One trick to Giraffe Listening is just to be . . . .
     T L S N E I

Food is a need. Broccoli is a . . . .
     A Y T T E S R G

Happy, sad, hurt, excited, and surprised are examples of . . . .
     G I E N E L S F

Giraffes are careful not to mix their feelings and their . . . .
     S H O H U G T T

You will be able to hear what is in another person's heart when you . . . .
     I N T E L S

GIRAFFE GAME:
WHAT CAN I SAY WHEN...?

Sometimes people say things to us and we don't know what to say back. You can try to guess what that person is needing and feeling. To practice, **take Blame Game words and match it to its possible Giraffe Game reply.**

BLAME GAME
WHEN SOMEONE SAYS TO ME....

GIRAFFE GAME
I CAN REPLY...

You're stupid.

You're a bully.

You're smart.

You're lazy.

You're a liar.

What's wrong with you?

Go away!

- Are you feeling disappointed because I didn't help and you're needing some teamwork?

- Are you feeling frustrated because I don't understand this game and you're needing some cooperation?

- Did you feel scared when I threw that ball at you and you're needing to be safe?

- Are you feeling confused and needing to understand the choices that I made?

- Are you mad and needing some space?

- Are you having a hard time trusting what I'm saying and are needing more information?

- Are you feeling happy that I figured this out and needing to celebrate?

GIRAFFE REQUESTS

Step 4 of the giraffe game is making requests.

A REQUEST: is a specific, do-able action another person can take in the present—right here, right now. With a request, the person is ok with hearing "no" as a reply.

A DEMAND: is a threat that something unpleasant might happen if the person doesn't do it. With a demand, they're not willing to hear "no."

A WISH: is when it's not clear what the person wants others to do or when they want them to do it.

Request Test

Circle either "Request" or "Demand" or "Wish"
depending on what you think each statement is.

1. If you don't clean up your room you won't be able to play after supper
   Request   Demand   Wish

2. Are you willing to hear my ideas on what activity to do next?
   Request   Demand   Wish

3. Is there any peanut butter?
   Request   Demand   Wish

4. Would it work for you to make supper while I clean the table?
   Request   Demand   Wish

5. Can you tell me how you feel about what I just said?
   Request   Demand   Wish

6. Put your coat on right now or else you can't go to show.
   Request   Demand   Wish

7. I wish I knew where my skateboard was.
   Request   Demand   Wish

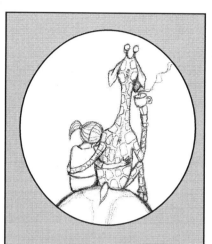

DID YOU KNOW…

"In the Malay peninsula in Southeast Asia, there is an aboriginal group called the Semai. The Semai are known for their non-violent attitudes. In their society it is very easy to say "no." The children of Semai are taught from an early age the concept of "bood." If a parent asks a child to do something and the child replies "I bood," in other words, "I don't feel like doing that," the matter is closed. The parent never tries to force the child to do something it does not want to do. As a consequence, Semai society has no formal leaders, no police, courts or government…and best of all, there is no violence.

DECODE THE SPECIAL MESSAGE

Fill in the blank beside each saying with the letter that best describes what kind of statement it is.
Then read all the letters together to find the secret giraffe message.

___ Stop doing that.

___ He got a 90 on the test.

___ I have a need for trust.

___ I feel ignored.

___ I'm thirsty.

I

___ I need a ride to school.

H

___ I am sad.

___ Your jacket is red.

___ Are you willing to be
flexible?

P

___ He is mean.

A

C

___ you are a liar.

J

U

___ I need a ride to school.

___ I feel you are mad at me.

B

___ That teacher is really lame.

P

___ You don't take life seriously.

A

C

___ She's so cool.

___ I feel excited.

U

L

O = OBSERVATIONS (Exactly what happened)	
E = EVALUATION (A judgment)	
F = FEELINGS (True feeling)	
T = THOUGHTS (False feelings, for eg. "I feel abused.")	
N = NEEDS (Universal needs we all share)	
S = STRATEGIES (I need you to do the dishes)	
R = REQUESTS (Are you open to hearing no?)	
D = DEMANDS (Said like there is no choice)	
W = WISHES (It's not clear what is being asked for)	

PUTTING IT ALL TOGETHER

Here are the four steps of Giraffe Language all in one place.

Step 1	OBSERVATION	When you _____
Step 2	FEELING	I feel _____ (see feelings on next page)
Step 3	NEED	Because I need _____ (see needs list next page)
Step 4	REQUEST	Are you willing to _____ ?

An easy way to remember this is to remember the first letters of the steps OFNR (pronounced off-ner).

PRACTICE.
HAVE FUN.
SPREAD PEACE.

INTERNATIONAL CENTER FOR NONVIOLENT COMMUNICATION

The Center for Nonviolent Communication (CNVC) is a global organization whose vision is a world where all people are getting their needs met and resolving their conflicts peacefully. In this vision, people are using Nonviolent Communication (NVC, referred to as "Giraffe Language" in this book) to create and participate in networks of worldwide life-serving systems in economics, education, justice, healthcare and peace-keeping.

Nonviolent Communication training evolved from Dr. Marshall Rosenberg's quest to find a way of rapidly disseminating much-needed peacemaking skills. The Center for Nonviolent Communication emerged out of work he was doing with civil rights activists in the early 1960s. During this period, he provided mediation and communication skills training to communities working to peacefully desegregate schools and other public institutions.

Since the center's inception, the response to Nonviolent Communication training has been extremely positive. It is seen as a powerful tool for peacefully resolving differences at personal, professional and political levels.

To learn more, visit www.cnvc.org online.

© 2009 by Center for Nonviolent Communication
www.cnvc.org. E-mail: cnvc@cnvc.org
Phone: +1-505-244-4041

NEEDS

Partial List of Giraffe Needs

CONNECTION
acceptance
affection
appreciation
belonging
cooperation
communication
closeness
community
companionship
compassion
consideration
consistency
empathy
inclusion
intimacy
love
mutuality
nurturing
respect
self-respect
safety
security
stability
support
to know
to be known
to see
to be seen
to understand
to be understood
trust
warmth

AUTONOMY
choice
freedom
independence
space
spontaneity

**PHYSICAL
WELL-BEING**
air
food
movement
exercise
rest/sleep
sexual expression
safety
shelter
touch
water

PEACE
beauty
communion
ease
equality
harmony
inspiration
order

MEANING
awareness
celebration of life
challenge
clarity
competence
consciousness
contribution
creativity
discovery
efficacy
effectiveness
growth
hope
learning
mourning
participation
purpose
self-expression
stimulation
to matter
understanding

HONESTY
authenticity
integrity
presence

PLAY
joy
humor

what's in your heart?

FEELINGS

Feelings when your needs are satisfied

AFFECTIONATE
compassionate
friendly
loving
open hearted
sympathetic
tender
warm

CONFIDENT
empowered
open
proud
safe
secure

ENGAGED
absorbed
alert
curious
engrossed
enchanted
entranced
fascinated
interested
intrigued
involved
spellbound
stimulated

GRATEFUL
appreciative
moved
thankful
touched

EXCITED
amazed
animated
ardent
aroused
astonished
dazzled
eager
energetic
enthusiastic
giddy
invigorated
lively
passionate
surprised
vibrant

EXHILARATED
blissful
ecstatic
elated
enthralled
exuberant
radiant
rapturous
thrilled

INSPIRED
amazed
awed
wonder

HOPEFUL
expectant
encouraged
optimistic

JOYFUL
amused
delighted
glad
happy
jubilant
pleased
tickled

PEACEFUL
calm
clear headed
comfortable
centered
content
equanimous
fulfilled
mellow
quiet
relaxed
relieved
satisfied
serene
still
tranquil
trusting

REFRESHED
enlivened
rejuvenated
renewed
rested
restored
revived

FEELINGS

Feelings when your needs are not satisfied

AFRAID	PAIN	DISQUIET	TENSE	DISCONNECTED
apprehensive	agony	Agitated	anxious	alienated
dread	anguished	alarmed	cranky	aloof
foreboding	bereaved	discombobulated	distressed	apathetic
frightened	devastated	disconcerted	distraught	bored
mistrustful	grief	disturbed	edgy	cold
panicked	heartbroken	perturbed	fidgety	detached
petrified	hurt	rattled	frazzled	distant
scared	lonely	restless	irritable	distracted
suspicious	miserable	shocked	jittery	indifferent
terrified	regretful	startled	nervous	numb
wary	remorseful	surprised	overwhelmed	removed
worried		troubled	restless	uninterested
	SAD	turbulent	stressed out	withdrawn
ANNOYED	depressed	turmoil		gloomy
aggravated	dejected	uncomfortable	FATIGUED	heavy hearted
dismayed	despair	uneasy	beat	hopeless
disgruntled	despondent	unnerved	burnt out	melancholy
displeased	disappointed	unsettled	depleted	unhappy
exasperated	discouraged	upset	exhausted	wretched
frustrated	disheartened		lethargic	
impatient	forlorn	EMBARRASSED	listless	AVERSION
irritated		ashamed	sleepy	animosity
irked	CONFUSED	chagrined	tired	appalled
	ambivalent	flustered	weary	contempt
ANGRY	baffled	guilty	worn out	disgusted
enraged	bewildered	mortified		dislike
furious	dazed	self-conscious	VULNERABLE	hate
incensed	hesitant		fragile	horrified
indignant	lost	YEARNING	guarded	hostile
irate	mystified	envious	helpless	repulsed
livid	perplexed	jealous	insecure	
outraged	puzzled	longing	leery	
resentful	torn	nostalgic	reserved	
		pining	sensitive	
		wistful	shaky	

www.GiraffeJuice.com

Would you take action if you knew that your effort could significantly decrease violence in the lives of young people? What if it was easy, took around a minute of your time, and was free?

REQUEST: Please go to www.GiraffeJuice.com and send the full-color e-book of *Giraffe Juice* to one or more people whom you think would appreciate receiving it. It's free, will take less than a minute, and you can keep all your information confidential (i.e., name, e-mail address, etc.).

You'll be taking part in using the power of media and the Internet to spread the awareness of Giraffe Language around the world! Over time, your single action could result in hundreds...even thousands...of people becoming exposed to Nonviolent Communication (NVC) for the first time...REALLY!

Our vision is to distribute a million copies of *Giraffe Juice* to kids and adults throughout the world, in either its physical or e-book form, by January 1st 2012.

THE MILLION GIRAFFES PROJECT IS ON THE GO!

We have acquired charitable donations for the nonprofit distribution of *Giraffe Juice* to schools, libraries, and organizations all over the globe. Our intention is to participate in co-creating a planet where people are increasingly able to experience peace within themselves, their families, and in the world.

Knowing that there are big people and little people who shy away from academic approaches to learning, one of the intentions of *Giraffe Juice* is to share a fun and entertaining entryway into the heart of Giraffe Language. Its goal is not to teach Nonviolent Communication, but rather to offer a whimsical glimpse into the spirit of the work so anyone may choose to learn more if they feel inspired.

Is there a teacher, parent, or young person you would enjoy sharing this book with?

Would you enjoy knowing that your choice to share the free e-book with someone you care about inspired this person to begin practicing Nonviolent Communication with his or her family, school, or organization?

If yes, go to www.GiraffeJuice.com. It will take you less than a minute to send out the full-color version of *Giraffe Juice*, and you will have the choice to keep all of your information confidential.

Ninety percent of the proceeds from the sale of the physical book (at www.GiraffeJuice.com) will be allocated to spreading Giraffe Language throughout the world via the Million Giraffes Project. The remaining ten percent will be donated to the Center for Nonviolent Communication to support its social change and peace-making efforts.

The Million Giraffes Project will be posting its progress regularly so you can keep tabs on how quickly we are achieving our goals. If you feel inspired to support this project through service see next page for more clarity.
If you wish to make a charitable donation you can contact JP directly at:
jp@GiraffeJuice.com.

www.GiraffeJuice.com

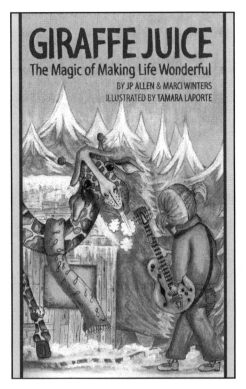

At GiraffeJuice.com you can:
- **Instantly and easily share the full-color e-book of Giraffe Juice with someone you care about (for free).**
- Purchase a physical copy of this book or its companion.

Giraffe Juice a story about Eva, a guitar-playing, harmonica-jamming girl who can make musical notes do wonders... but when it comes to getting Jip to stop bullying her at school, she doesn't know where to start. Then one day Eva discovers a secret.

As you will soon discover, some people like to use this secret to deal with people who bully. Giraffes like to use it to make life fun...because making life fun...for you and everyone...is their favorite game in town.

(Significant discounts available for the purchase of multiple copies.)

At www.GiraffeJuice.com you can also find out how to get:
- Free copies of *Giraffe Juice* to share with your school
- Giraffe games, puppets, and ears.

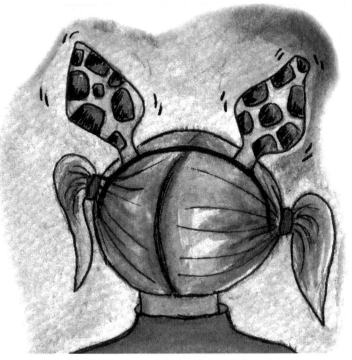

www.GiraffeJuice.com

ARE YOU A PARENT OR A TEACHER NEEDING SUPPORT?

At www.GiraffeJuice.com you will find:

- Parent/teacher forums where you can connect with others and request support
- Info about giraffe schools/camps
- A complete learning guide of NVC books, videos, CD's, and other resources

PLEASE COME AND POST YOUR PROJECT ON GIRAFFEJUICE.COM!

At GiraffeJuice.com you will be able to easily post any NVC-related projects, resources or individual missions that you would like to share with others. You are also welcomed to post projects and resources not specific to NVC, if you are confident they will support parents, teachers, and kids in deepening their Giraffe skills.

WOULD YOU ENJOY CO-CREATING THE SEQUEL?

We're already planning the sequel to *Giraffe Juice* to better serve its mission in the world...if you are a best-selling author or editor of kids' books and are very confident with your NVC skills, we would love to work with you. We're also looking to hire highly experienced professionals with the following skills: developmental editing, plot development, web development, marketing, and workbook development (please respond only if you feel extremely confident with your NVC skills). Contact jp@giraffejuice.com.

THE MILLION GIRAFFES PROJECT WOULD LOVE YOUR SUPPORT.

If you feel uneasy about your Giraffe skills, there are still many ways to contribute. Firstly, e-mailing the free e-book of Giraffe Juice to as many people as possible will be an enormous contribution. Secondly, we would love to hire people with the following skills: project management, web design, marketing, distribution, proofreading, voice-over (for the audio book), music, visual art, graphic art, and school administration. If you're interested in connecting with us, or making a charitable donation, write to jp@GiraffeJuice.com.

AN EXCERPT FROM GIRAFFE JUICE

Oh, by the way," she went on, half out of breath, "I made an appointment with Principal Pickle on Tuesday afternoon to meet about the Giraffe Club. But I'm afraid that he won't want to hear a word I say. Do you have any ideas?"

"What is it exactly that you want to get out of the meeting?" Marvel asked thoughtfully.

"I want Principal Pickle to approve the Giraffe Club! That's all I care about."

Marvel snorted, "I'm concerned that if you go into the meeting trying only to get your way, and not caring equally about Principal Pickle's needs, he may not approve the project…even if he actually likes it."

"Well then how do I make him believe that I care about his needs?"

"It really doesn't matter how you do it. What matters most is that you really do care about his needs."

Marvel lowered his voice to a whisper, "What I'm about to tell you may really help."

Eva closed her eyes, ready to drink in his words.

"Approach Principal Pickle with an open heart. Rather than trying to get your own way, listen for *his* needs. If he senses that you really care about his needs, he might start caring about yours. Then whole new solutions can become possible."

Eva put her hand on her forehead. "The truth is that, right now, I don't care about Principal Pickle. I don't think he'll take me or the club seriously."

"Are you feeling hopeless that he won't care about what matters to you?"

"Yeah. Grown-ups only care about grown-up stuff. I don't think he really cares about my needs. So how am I supposed to care about him?"

"Listen deeper. See if you can find ways that he is the same as you. Beneath everything Principal Pickle thinks, feels, or does, he is motivated by the same things you care about. Just like you, he has needs for fun, celebration and the love of friends and family.

"I know you may not like all the things Principal Pickle does, but if you turn your attention to the part of him that is the same as you, it will be easier to find space in your heart to care about his needs."

Eva nodded. "I've thought about this, but I've never heard it put in quite those words."

Marvel continued, "I believe that deep inside every person is a natural spirit that wants to take care of life: the life inside of other people and the life in all living things. This caring could be as simple as helping to cook a meal, planting trees, or recycling. Or it could be as big as protecting the rainforests.

"There are so many ways to care about life. When I know that my actions have made others' lives more wonderful, I get a surge of energy. I call that energy GIRAFFE JUICE. It's a magical energy that juices me up and makes me feel alive.

"Sometimes it tingles happily like a jolt of electricity. Sometimes it flows steadily through me, making me feel warm and wonderful…but whatever this energy is, it gives me the power to go out and keep helping others."

"Speaking of helping others…" Eva dipped her hand into her pocket and pulled out a big bandage. She smiled. "I thought you might need a new one for the cut on your leg." Marvel placed his front hoof delicately in Eva's hands.

Eva had a big sunny smile on her face for the entire time she was wrapping the bandage around Marvel's leg.

"I think I get what you're saying, Marvel. Because I'm alive, there's a part of me that naturally wants to take care of life. It's almost like me and all living things are in the same family. Is that what you're saying, Marvel?"

When she noticed him looking at her peacefully, she stopped. Her eyes got wide with delight. "I FEEL IT, MARVEL!"

"What, Eva?"

"The juice, Marvel! I FEEL GIRAFFE JUICE!"

ANSWER KEY

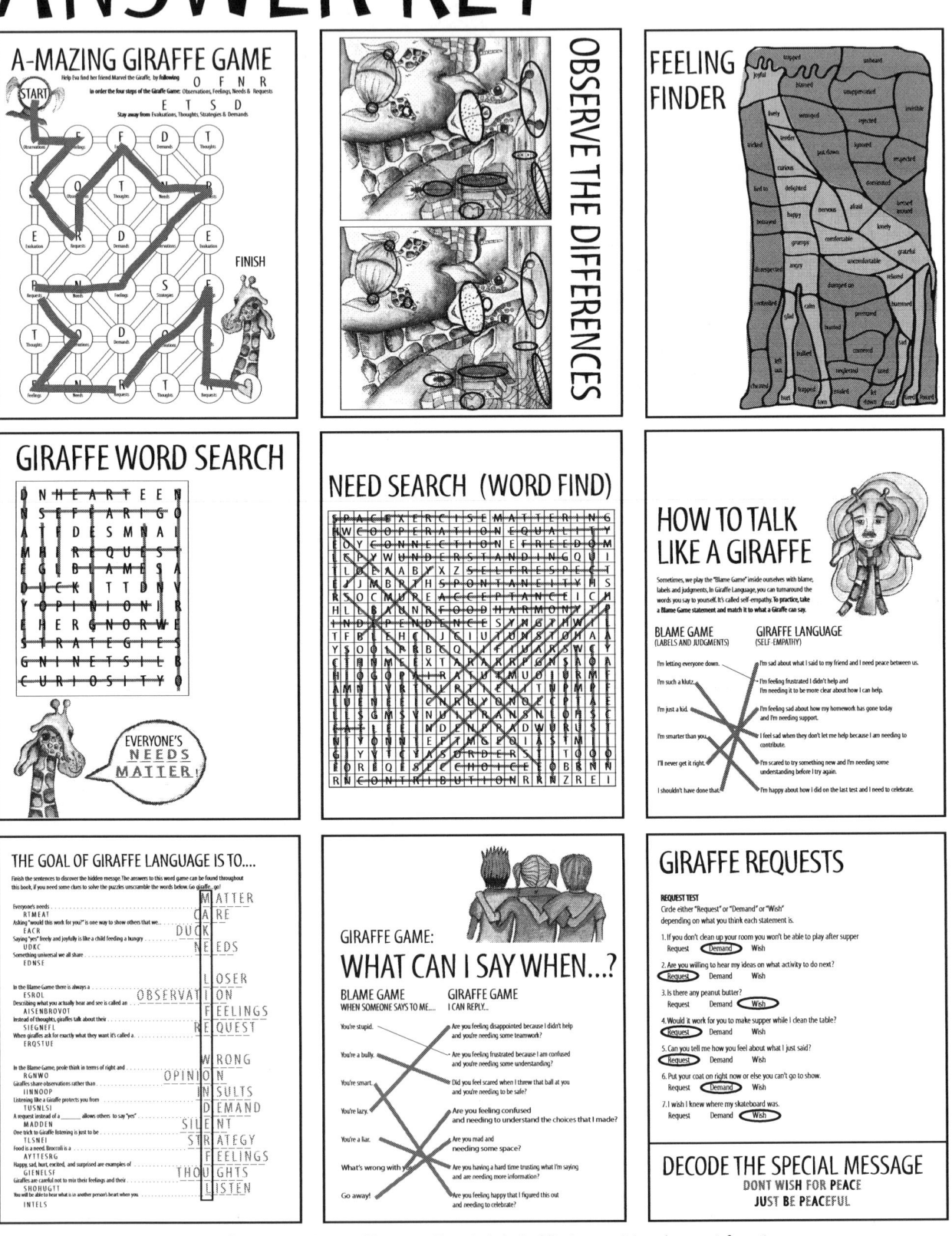

A-MAZING GIRAFFE GAME

Help Eva find her friend Marvel the Giraffe, by following **O F N R** in order the four steps of the Giraffe Game: Observations, Feelings, Needs & Requests. Stay away from **E T S D** Evaluations, Thoughts, Strategies & Demands.

START ... FINISH

OBSERVE THE DIFFERENCES

FEELING FINDER

GIRAFFE WORD SEARCH

EVERYONE'S NEEDS MATTER!

NEED SEARCH (WORD FIND)

HOW TO TALK LIKE A GIRAFFE

Sometimes, we play the "Blame Game" inside ourselves with blame, labels and judgments. In Giraffe Language, you can turnaround the words you say to yourself. It's called self-empathy. To practice, take a Blame Game statement and match it to what a Giraffe can say.

BLAME GAME (LABELS AND JUDGMENTS)

- I'm letting everyone down.
- I'm such a klutz.
- I'm just a kid.
- I'm smarter than you.
- I'll never get it right.
- I shouldn't have done that.

GIRAFFE LANGUAGE (SELF-EMPATHY)

- I'm sad about what I said to my friend and I need peace between us.
- I'm feeling frustrated I didn't help and I'm needing it to be more clear about how I can help.
- I'm feeling sad about how my homework has gone today and I'm needing support.
- I feel sad when they don't let me help because I am needing to contribute.
- I'm scared to try something new and I'm needing some understanding before I try again.
- I'm happy about how I did on the last test and I need to celebrate.

THE GOAL OF GIRAFFE LANGUAGE IS TO....

Finish the sentences to discover the hidden message. The answers to this word game can be found throughout this book. If you need some clues to solve the puzzles unscramble the words below. Go giraffe, go!

Clue	Answer
Everyone's needs .... RTMEAT	MATTER
Asking "would this work for you?" is one way to show others that we... EACR	CARE
Saying "yes" freely and joyfully is like a child feeding a hungry ... UDKC	DUCK
Something universal we all share ..... EDNSF	NEEDS
In the Blame Game there is always a ... ESROL	LOSER
Describing what you actually hear and see is called an ... AISENBROVOT	OBSERVATION
Instead of thoughts, giraffes talk about their ... SIEGNEFL	FEELINGS
When giraffes ask for exactly what they want it's called a ... ERQSTUE	REQUEST
In the Blame Game, people think in terms of right and ... RGNWO	WRONG
Giraffes share observations rather than ... IINNOOP	OPINION
Listening like a Giraffe protects you from ... TUSMLSI	INSULTS
A request instead of a ___ allows others to say "yes" ... MADDEN	DEMAND
One trick to Giraffe listening is just to be ... TLSNEI	SILENT
Food is a need. Broccoli is a ... AYTTESRG	STRATEGY
Happy, sad, hurt, excited, and surprised are examples of ... GIENELSF	FEELINGS
Giraffes are careful not to mix their feelings and their ... SHOHUGTT	THOUGHTS
You will be able to hear what is in another person's heart when you ... INTELS	LISTEN

GIRAFFE GAME: WHAT CAN I SAY WHEN...?

BLAME GAME WHEN SOMEONE SAYS TO ME...

- You're stupid.
- You're a bully.
- You're smart.
- You're lazy.
- You're a liar.
- What's wrong with you?
- Go away!

GIRAFFE GAME I CAN REPLY...

- Are you feeling disappointed because I didn't help and you're needing some teamwork?
- Are you feeling frustrated because I am confused and you're needing some understanding?
- Did you feel scared when I threw that ball at you and you're needing to be safe?
- Are you feeling confused and needing to understand the choices that I made?
- Are you mad and needing some space?
- Are you having a hard time trusting what I'm saying and are needing more information?
- Are you feeling happy that I figured this out and needing to celebrate?

GIRAFFE REQUESTS

REQUEST TEST

Circle either "Request" or "Demand" or "Wish" depending on what you think each statement is.

1. If you don't clean up your room you won't be able to play after supper — **Demand**
2. Are you willing to hear my ideas on what activity to do next? — **Request**
3. Is there any peanut butter? — **Wish**
4. Would it work for you to make supper while I clean the table? — **Request**
5. Can you tell me how you feel about what I just said? — **Request**
6. Put your coat on right now or else you can't go to show. — **Demand**
7. I wish I knew where my skateboard was. — **Wish**

DECODE THE SPECIAL MESSAGE

DON'T WISH FOR PEACE
JUST BE PEACEFUL

Made in the USA
San Bernardino, CA
19 June 2018